TRINITY
COLLEGE LONDON PRESS

GW00493415

INITIAL-GRADE 02
ACOUSTIC GUITAR

Fingerstyle & Plectrum Pieces
for Trinity College London
Exams 2020-2023

 Free downloads

Published by
Trinity College London Press Ltd
trinitycollege.com

Registered in England
Company no. 09726123

Initial Unaccompanied *or* with backing

Count in

Ain't No Sunshine

Bill Withers
arr. Rye

Steadily ♩ = 80

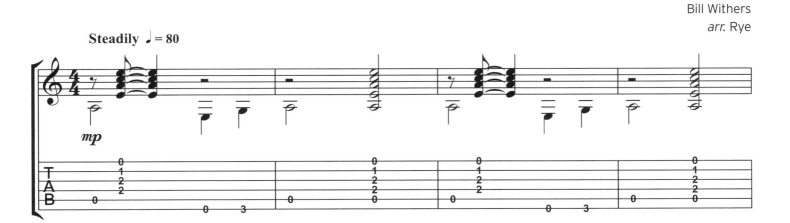

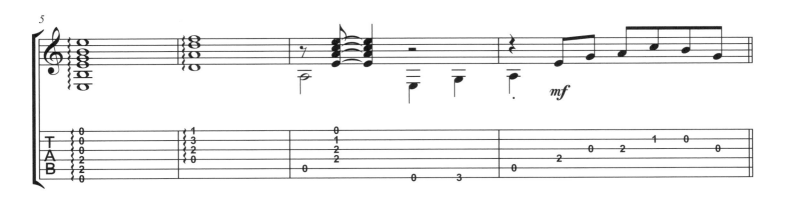

Count in
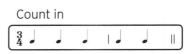

Amazing Grace

Newton
arr. Walker

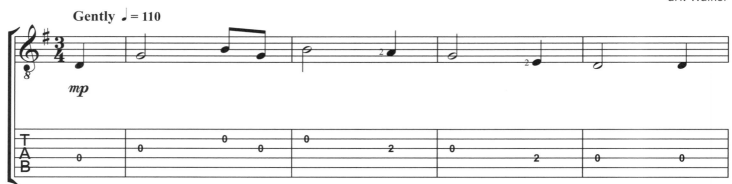

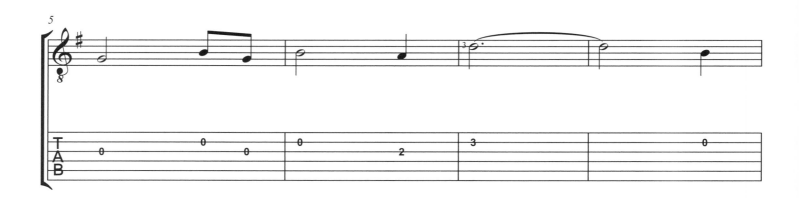

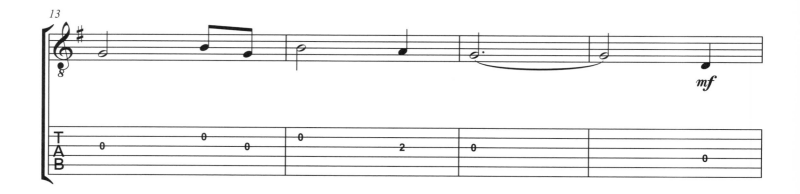

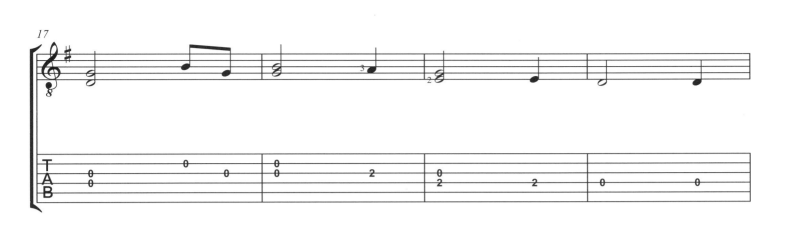

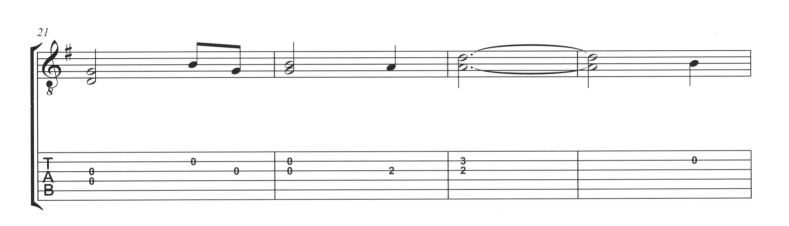

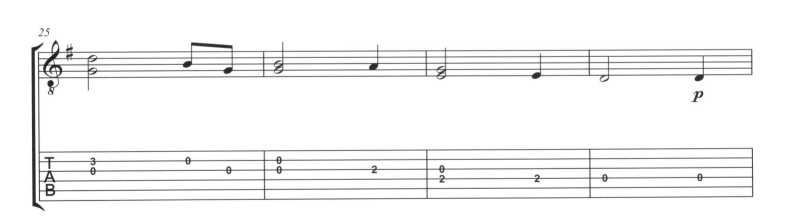

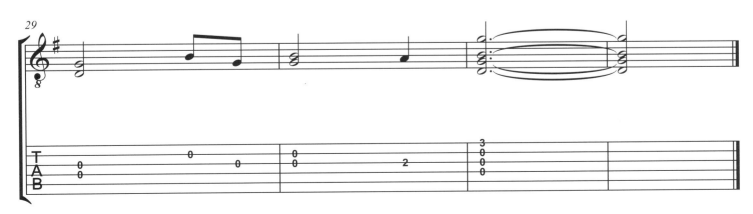

Count in

Oh When the Saints

Trad.
arr. Walker

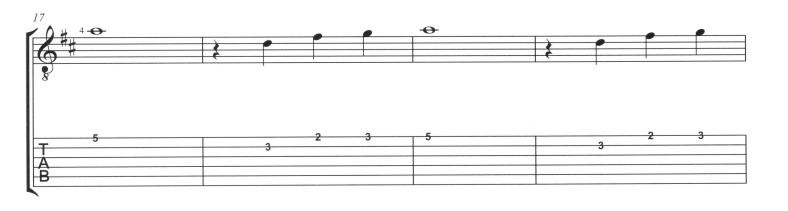

7

Count in

Redemption Song

Bob Marley
arr. Walker

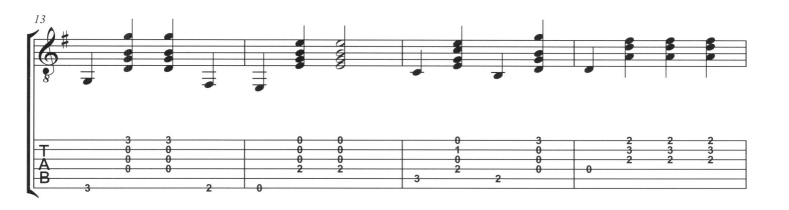

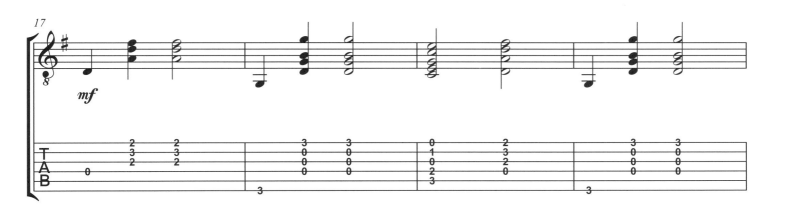

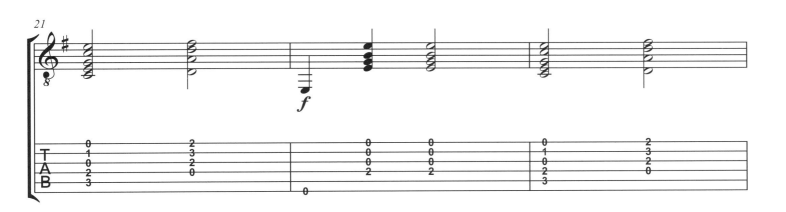

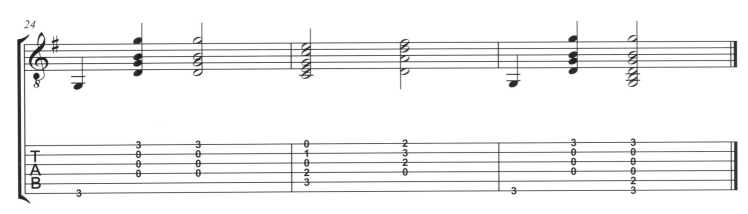

Rockin' the Country

Brett Duncan

Notes

Stegosaurus Strut

Nick Powlesland

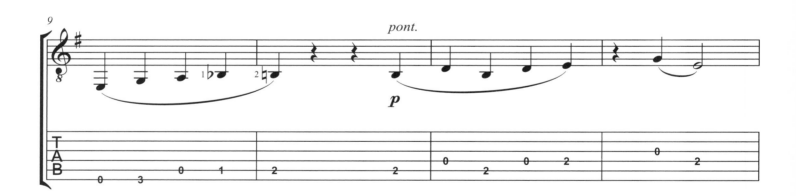

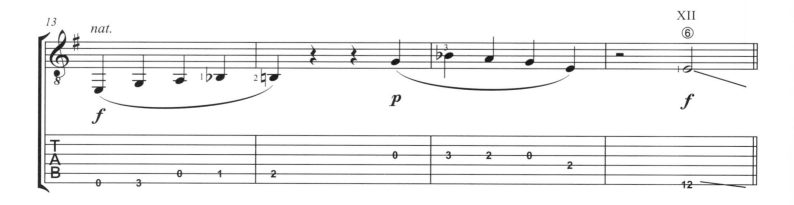

Count in

Summer Rain

T J Walker

Candidate part

Duet part

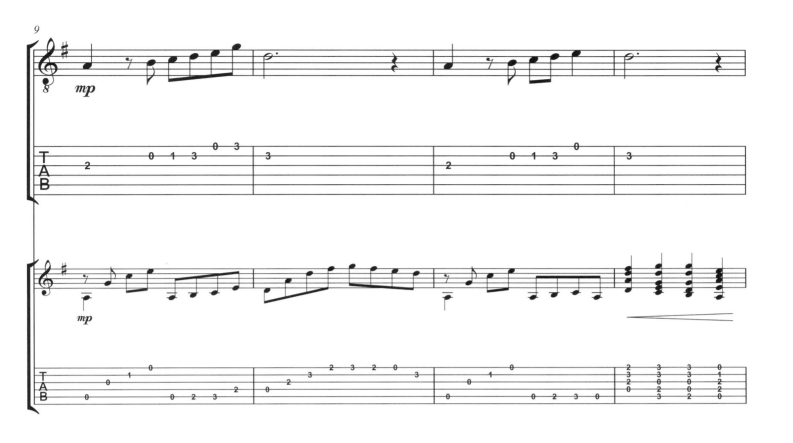

Surfin' Safari

Brian Wilson & Mike Love

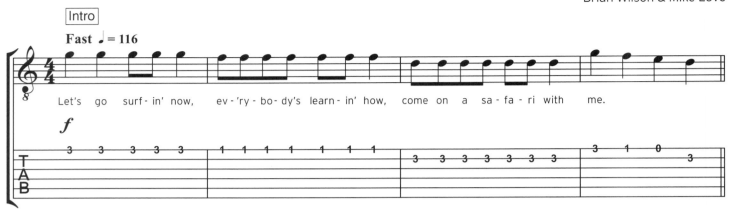

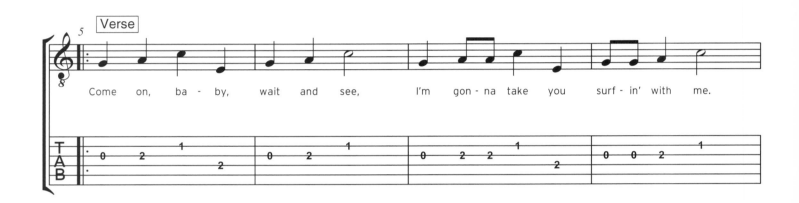

Initial Unaccompanied *or* with backing

Count in

White Windmill

T J Walker

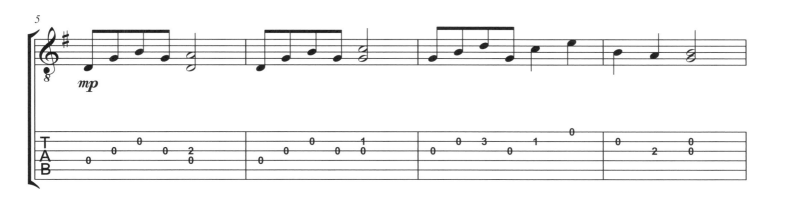

17

Notes

Grade 1 Unaccompanied *or* with backing

Count in

Cuba Kick!

Tim Pells

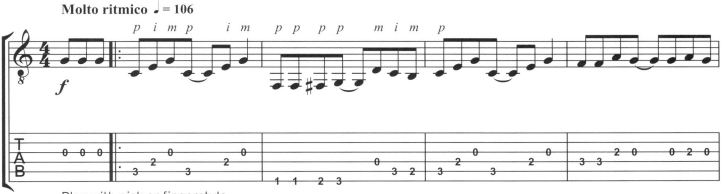

Play with pick or fingerstyle

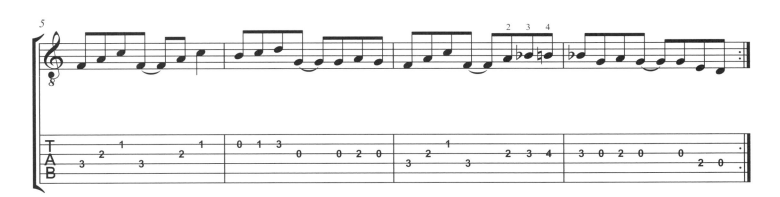

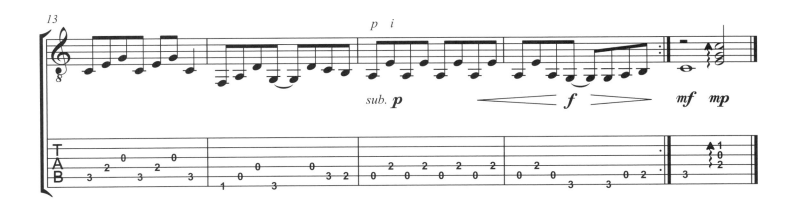

A Fistful of Pesos

Nick Powlesland

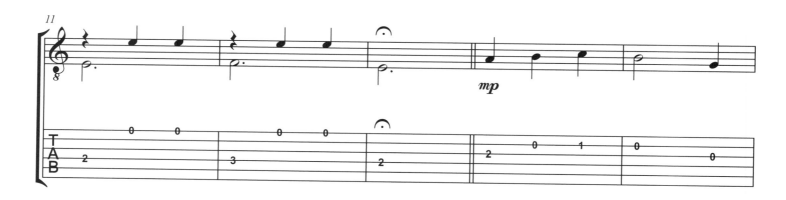

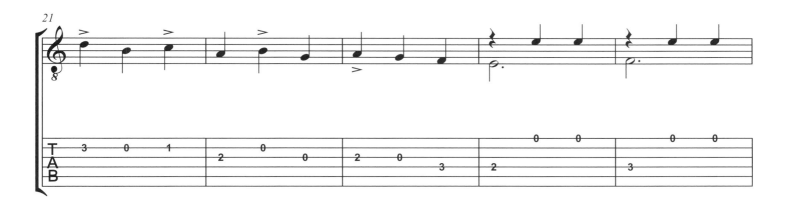

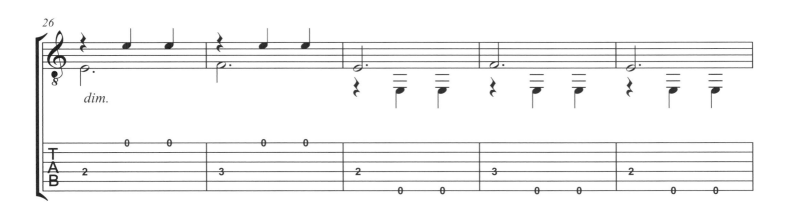

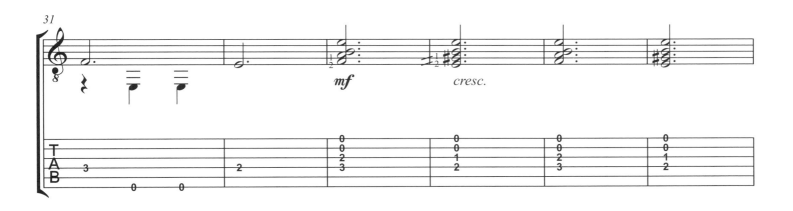

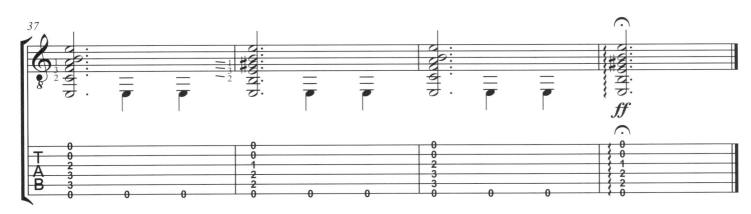

The Hungry Ghost

Leslie Searle

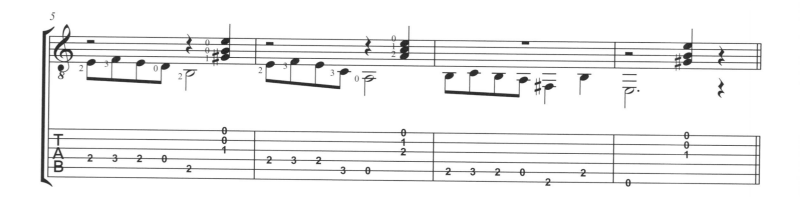

Notes

Count in

Perfect Sky

T J Walker

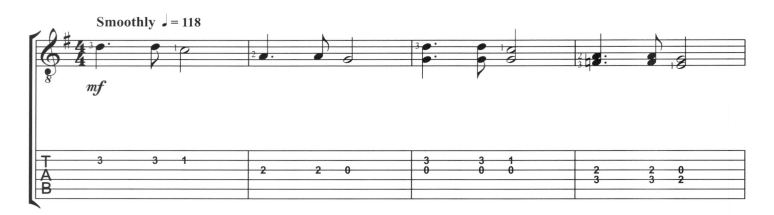

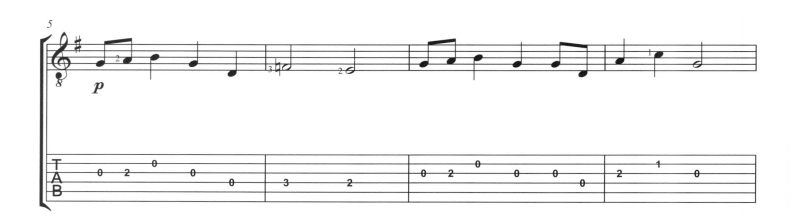

Grade 1 Backing required for exam

Count in
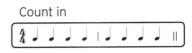

Photograph

John McDaid, Ed Sheeran,
Tom Leonard & Martin Harrington

arr. Rye

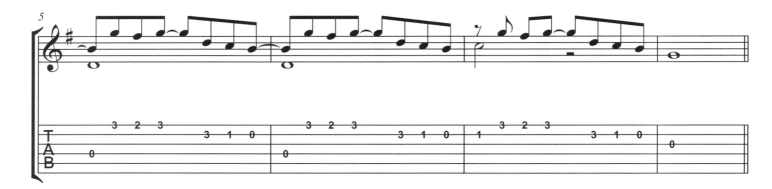

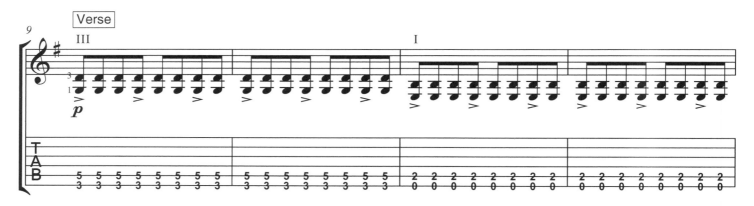

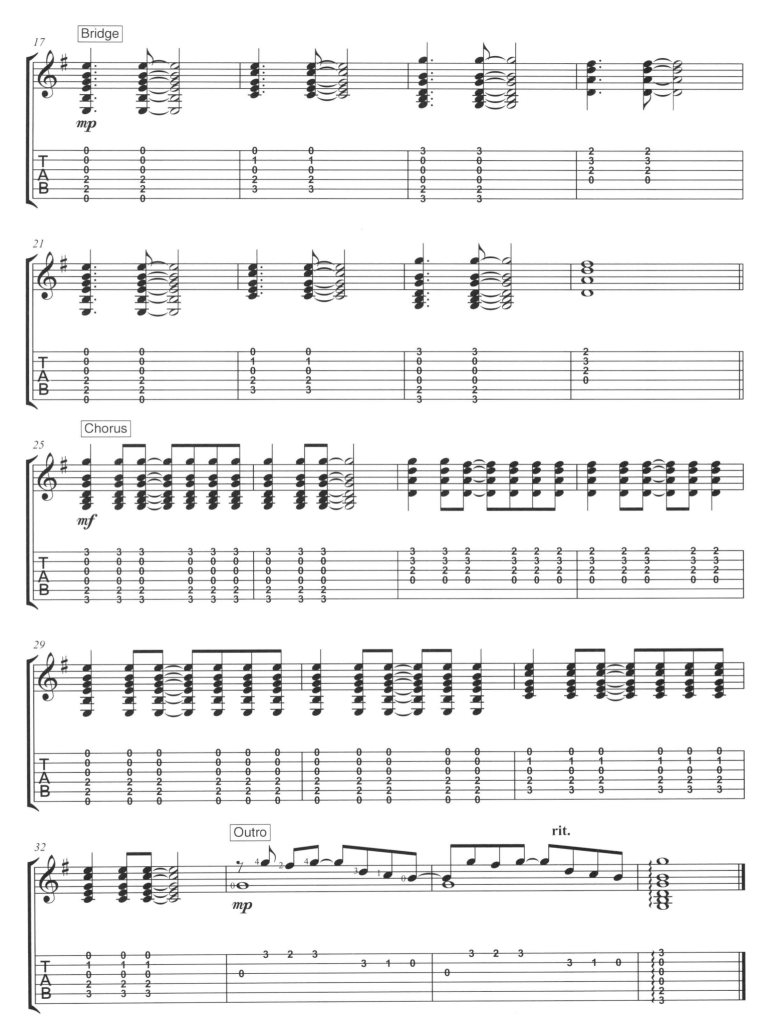

Sailor's Hornpipe

Trad.
arr. Burden

Notes

A Tale of the Green Isle

Robert Morandell

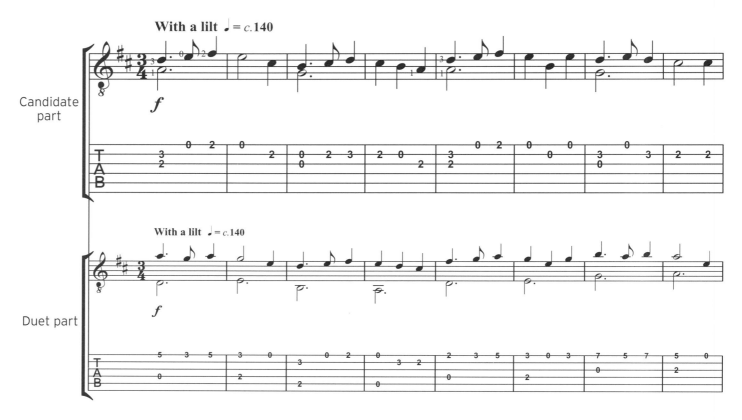

D.S. al Fine

D.S. al Fine

Count in

Tango Memories

Tim Pells

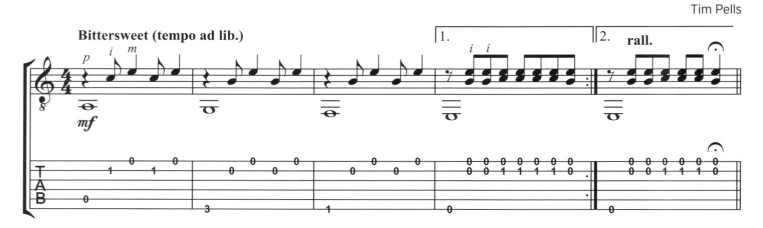

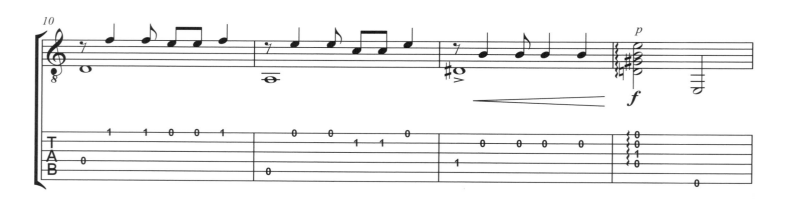

poco rall.

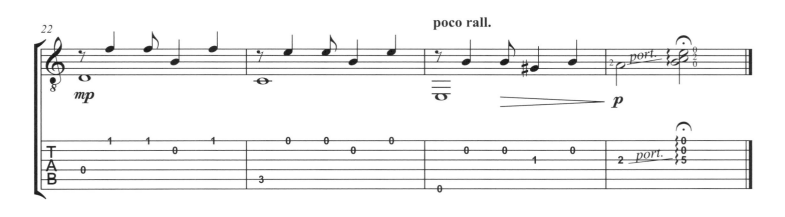

Count in

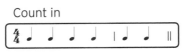

Waterloo Sunset

Ray Davies
arr. Walker

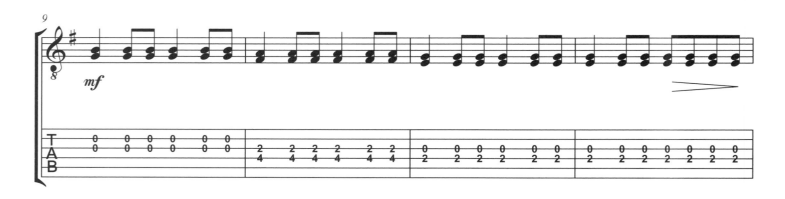

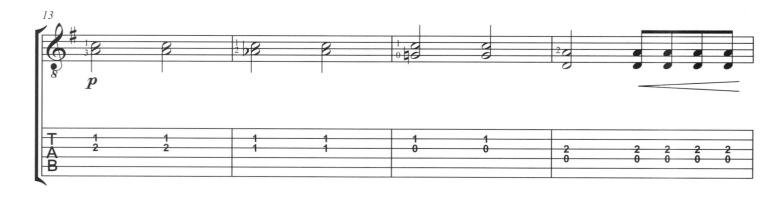

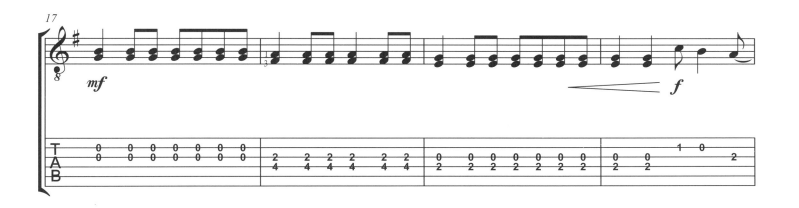

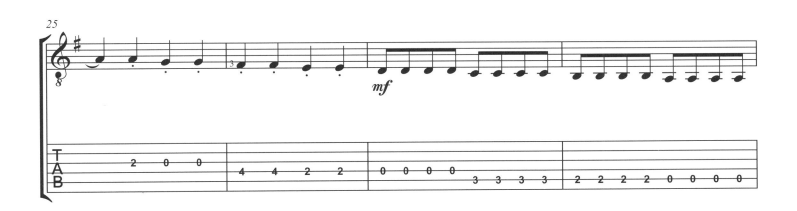

Bad Jack

Nick Powlesland

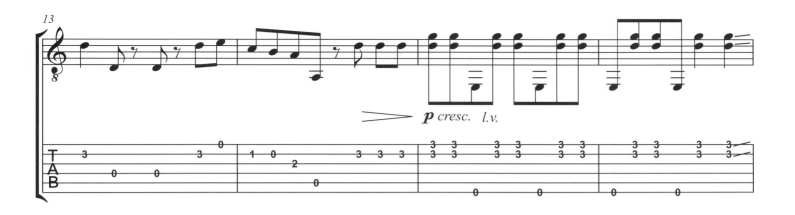

Count in

Blue Rag

Robert Morandell

Candidate part

Duet part

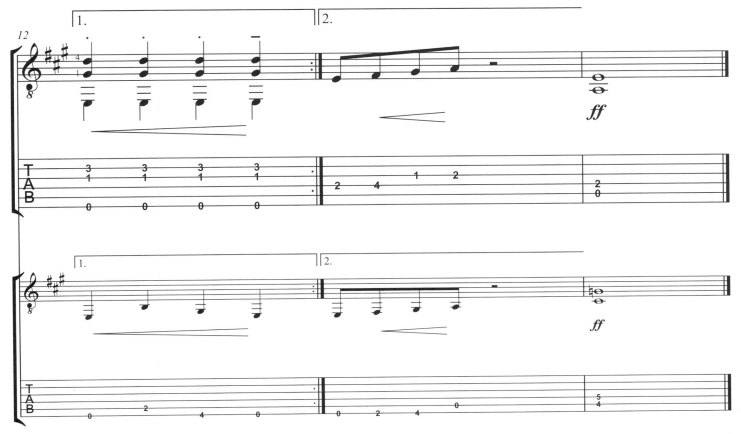

House of the Rising Sun

Trad.
arr. Pells

With a melancholy feel ♩ = 108

Jamaica

Nick Powlesland

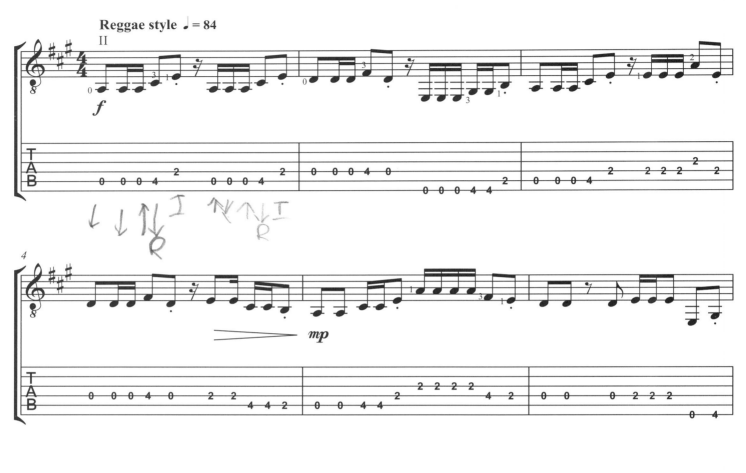

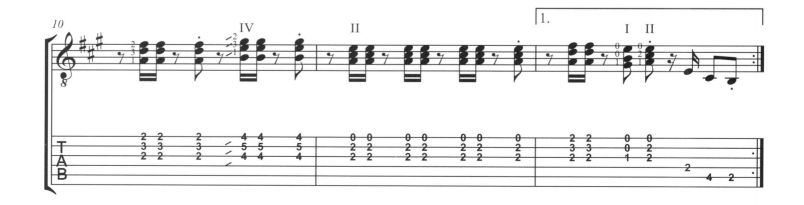

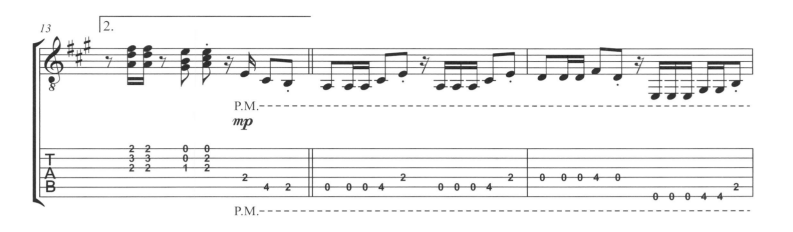

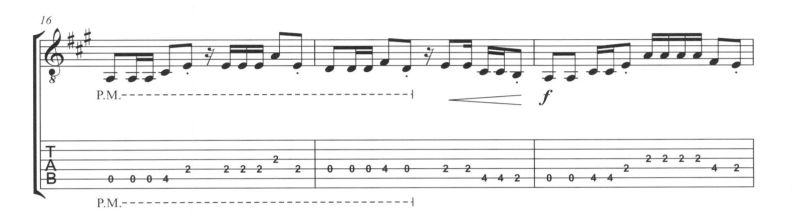

New Memory Lane

Tim Pells

44

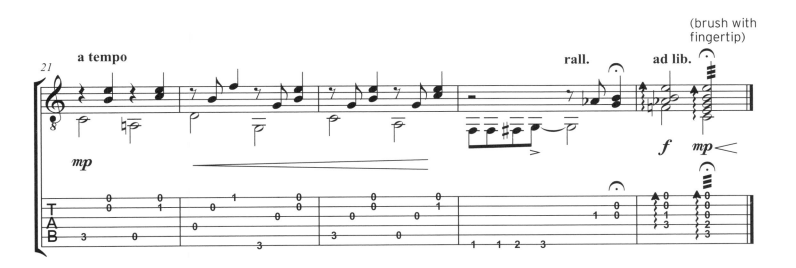

Count in

Rockodile Reggae

Robert Morandell

Notes

Count in

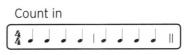

Sail Away

T J Walker

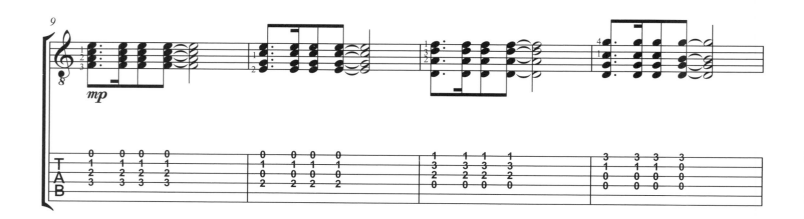

Turkey in the Straw

Trad.
arr. Fred Sokolow

Count in

What a Wonderful World

Thiele & Weiss
arr. Walker

Intro

Smoothly ♩. = 73

Verse

½CIV

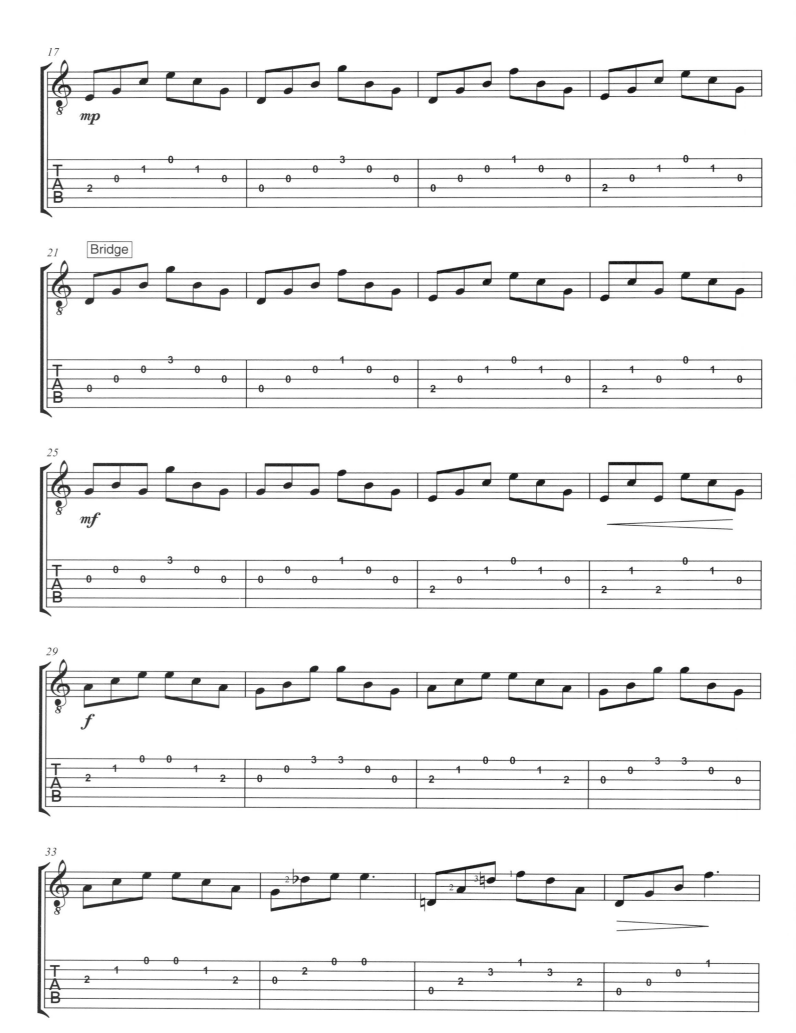

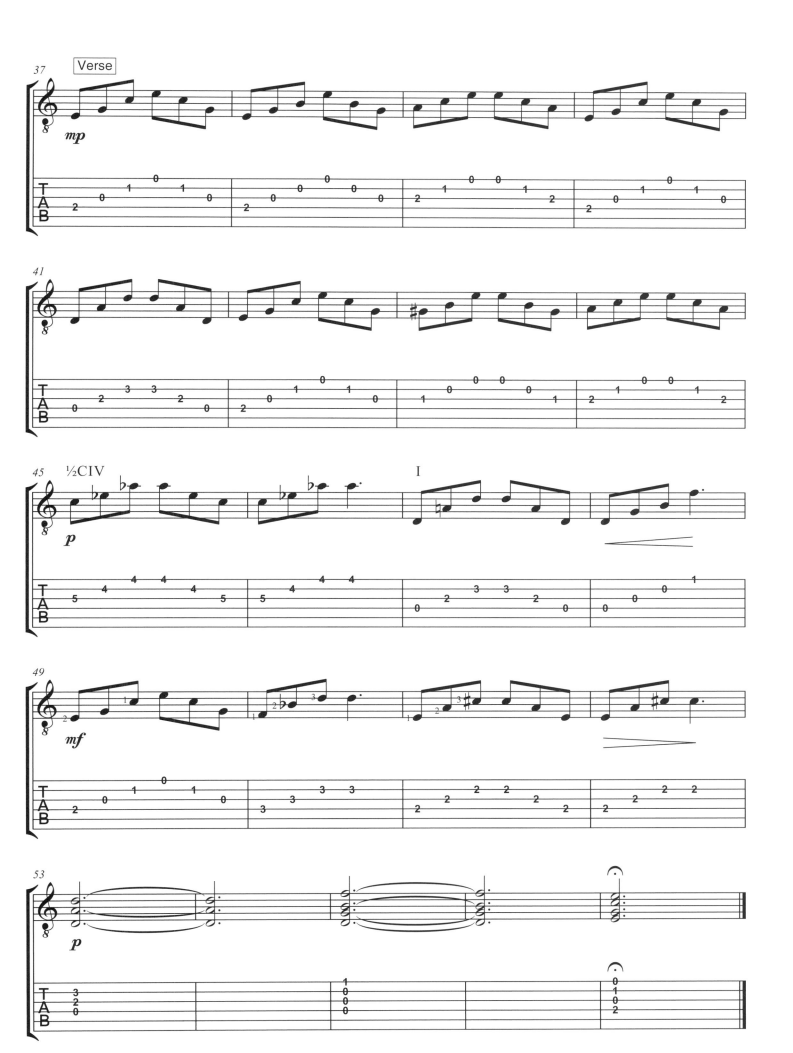

Notes

Notes

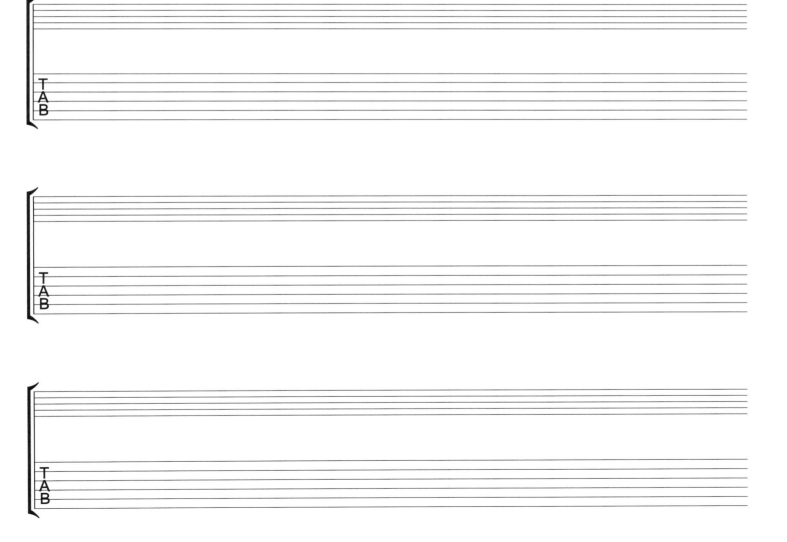

Recording credits

Initial

Ain't No Sunshine   Bill Withers, *arr.* Rye
Acoustic Guitar & Bass Guitar: T J Walker • Programming: T J Walker

Amazing Grace   Newton, *arr.* Walker
Acoustic Guitar, Bass Guitar, Hammond & Piano: T J Walker • Programming: T J Walker

Oh When the Saints   Trad., *arr.* Walker
Acoustic Guitar, Bass Guitar & Piano: T J Walker • Programming: T J Walker

Redemption Song   Bob Marley, *arr.* Walker
Acoustic Guitar, Bass Guitar, Hammond & Vocals: T J Walker • Programming: T J Walker

Summer Rain   T J Walker
Acoustic Guitars: T J Walker • Programming: T J Walker

White Windmill   T J Walker
Acoustic Guitar, Bass Guitar & Piano: T J Walker • Programming: T J Walker

Grade 1

Cuba Kick!   Pells
Acoustic Guitar, Bass Guitar, Piano & Percussion: T J Walker • Programming: T J Walker

Perfect Sky   T J Walker
Acoustic Guitar, Bass Guitar & Piano: T J Walker • Programming: T J Walker

Photograph   Ed Sheeran (with McDaid, Leonard & Harrington), *arr.* Rye
Acoustic Guitar, Bass Guitar, Piano & Vocals: T J Walker • Programming: T J Walker

A Tale of the Green Isle   Morandell
Acoustic Guitars: Simon Hurley

Tango Memories   Pells
Acoustic Guitar & Bass Guitar: T J Walker • Programming: T J Walker

Waterloo Sunset   The Kinks (Davies), *arr.* Walker
Acoustic Guitar, Electric Guitar, Bass Guitar & Vocals: T J Walker • Programming: T J Walker

Grade 2

Blue Rag   Morandell
Acoustic Guitars: T J Walker

House of the Rising Sun   Trad., *arr.* Pells
Acoustic Guitar: Simon Hurley

New Memory Lane   Pells
Acoustic Guitar: Simon Hurley

Rockodile Reggae   Morandell
Acoustic Guitar, Bass Guitar, Hammond & Percussion: T J Walker • Programming: T J Walker

Sail Away   T J Walker
Acoustic Guitar, Bass Guitar & Piano: T J Walker • Programming: T J Walker

What a Wonderful World   Louis Armstrong (Thiele & Weiss), *arr.* Walker
Acoustic Guitar, Piano & Vocals: T J Walker • Programming: T J Walker

Tracks recorded, mixed and mastered by T J Walker **iamtjwalker.com**